THE COUNCIL OF HEAVEN

—A DRAMATIC POEM—

> Cover Art
>
> *Le combat de Jacob et L'Ange,* 1855-61
>
> (Jacob Wrestles with The Angel)
>
> fresco (detail) in Église Saint-Sulpice, Paris
>
> Eugene Delacroix (1798-1863)
>
> Gianni Dagli Orti / The Art Archive at Art Resource, NY

```
    V
    E
A R T
    S
    E
```

THE COUNCIL OF HEAVEN

—A DRAMATIC POEM—

An Allegory of Love, Human and Divine

Patricia Anne Kirby Craddock

2nd Edition

Copyright © 2014

Pontifex Press, LLC
Atlanta, Georgia

Copyright © 2010 and 2014 by Patricia Anne Kirby Craddock

All rights reserved. No part of this publication may be reproduced or transmitted in any form or by any means, electronic or mechanical, including photocopy, recording, or any information storage and retrieval system, without permission in writing from the publisher.

Pontifex Press, LLC, Atlanta, GA

Published in 2014 by Pontifex Press, LLC.
Distributed to the trade by Lulu Press, Inc.

Library of Congress Cataloguing-in-Publication Data
Craddock, Patricia Anne Kirby, 1923—
The council of heaven / Patricia Anne Kirby Craddock.
p. cm.

ISBN-10: 0-9913009-0-4
ISBN-13: 978-0-9913009-0-7

First published in the United States in 2010 in a limited hard cover edition by The Edwin Mellen Press, Lewiston, NY. Second edition published in 2014 by Pontifex Press, LLC, Atlanta, GA.

Visit Pontifex Press's website at www.PontifexPress.com

Book design and layout by Stephanie N. Bryan

Cover Art: *Le combat de Jacob et L'Ange,* 1855-61
by Eugene Delacroix (1798-1863)
fresco (detail) in Église Saint-Sulpice, Paris
Copyright © Gianni Dagli Orti / The Art Archive at Art Resource, NY

Printed in the United States of America

ACKNOWLEDGMENTS

Special thanks to Professor Herbert Richardson,
Director of The Edwin Mellen Press, Lewiston, NY,
for his valued guidance, on matters such as the title of this book.

Stanza No. 26 appeared, under the title "To Lisa",
In the Italian bimonthly publication
OggiFuturo, Organo Ufficiale
Dell'Accademia Internazionale
Dei Micenei, Reggio Calabria, Italy,
Anno XVII, No. 1, Gennaio-Aprile 2000.

DEDICATION

To my granddaughter Stephanie Nicole Bryan,
artist, writer, landscape architect, and photographer.
My collaborator *sans pareil* in Poetry and Art,
my ideal student of the world, my friend, my other self—
dreaming dreams for me I never dared to dream,
and, by your inspired vision and devoted labor,
making them come true!

THE COUNCIL OF HEAVEN

—A DRAMATIC POEM—

AN ALLEGORY OF LOVE—HUMAN AND DIVINE

With newly-human Satan as sinful man,

who—by God's grace and his own remorse—

may still have hope of Heaven!

*

An impassioned verbal Armageddon
at the end of the Millennium
on the eve of Revelation/Resurrection.
An ironic but deadly serious battle of wits
between **Lucifer**, Antichrist from Hell,
and a Band of Mortal Artists and Poets
newly returned by God to Earth:
**Dante, Michelangelo, Rembrandt, Goethe,
Milton, Shakespeare, and Leonardo,**
to convince Lucifer of the error of his ways,
perhaps even, thereby, to persuade God—
via His Holy Spirit's emissary from Heaven,
St. Francis of Assisi—
*to postpone the Day of Judgment
foretold in the Apocalypse!*

TIME: *Judgment Eve* PLACE: *The Earth*

DRAMATIC PERSONS
(in order of appearance)

SATAN/LUCIFER, Fallen Rebel Archangel

DANTE ALIGHIERI, Italian (Florentine) Poet

MICHELANGELO BUONARROTI, Sculptor, of Florence and Rome

REMBRANDT VAN RIJN, Painter from Leiden, the Netherlands

WILLIAM SHAKESPEARE, Dramatist, of Stratford-upon-Avon, England

JOHN MILTON, English Poet, from London

JOHANN WOLFGANG VON GOETHE, Philosopher/Playwright, of Frankfort, Germany

LEONARDO DA VINCI, Universal Italian Genius, also a Florentine

*   SPIRIT (Divine Intermediary)

Vittoria,   friend and patron to Michelangelo
Beatrice,   beloved of Dante
Christiane,   Goethe's wife
Mary,   Milton's first wife
Saskia,   Rembrandt's first wife
Anne,   Shakespeare's wife
Mona Lisa,   Leonardo's idealized inspiration

*   SAINT FRANCIS OF ASSISI   * (one and the same)

**   THE HOLY SPIRIT OF THE LORD   ** (voiced first and last, in Prologue/Epilogue)

THE LORD JESUS CHRIST
THE LORD GOD

(SCENE)

The setting, a rather stark landscape which—except for the gradually changing illuminations of twilight, midnight and dawn—remains the same throughout the poem-play, might be called the Graveyard of all Earth. As the protagonists appear, the voice of the Holy Spirit is heard impressing upon them the urgency of their individual roles in God's masterful, unfolding plan for Satan's reconciliation, through Man, with Himself. Gravestones, crypts and sarcophagi abound and on one of them Lucifer, newly mortal, elegantly reclines, pleasantly musing on the timeliness—on the very brink of Judgment—of this new and rare opportunity to re-tempt Man to linger on Earth indefinitely, together with himself, of course, God permitting—perhaps even to return to Hell! Listening cynically, he scarcely hears the Lord's commanding charge and certainly is not inclined to heed it.

He is a proud and worldly figure, darkly bearded and richly garbed, not unpleasing to the eye, but the old arrogant, contemptuous gleam escapes his jaded eye, still burdened as he is—despite his new God-given mantle of humanity—with the inward vision and knowledge of the fruits of good and evil of centuries. He is roused from his pleasant reverie by the approach of an all too familiar band of comely men who—all seeming in excellent health, voice and spirits, and clothed not in burial robes but at the height of their contemporary fashion—are saluting one another with kisses and embraces, with glad and joyful cries of recognition and affection.

Deciding to don at once his deceptive guise of innocent camaraderie with these favorite adversaries of himself and favored representatives of genius singled out by God, he rises in mocking but wary deference and respect, his glittering gaze and sharp, dissembling smile masking well his vague unease at greeting—on unprecedented equal footing—this superior band of artists and poets. They, in turn, stare in astonishment at the sight of Lucifer, human, whom all instinctively recognize as he stands jauntily before them, and they wonder—despite the divine injunction they too have just heard—at God's seemingly paradoxical purpose in first honoring them above all men by resurrecting them early, presumably to enter Heaven, on the *eve* of Judgment, and then sending Satan himself to welcome them back to Earth!

Minuit, Chrétiens, c'est l'Heure solennelle,
Où L'Homme Dieu descendit jusqu'à nous
Pour effacer la tache originelle
Et de Son Père arrêter le courroux.

—from *Cantique de Noel*, a French carol
composed by Adolphe Adam, 1847

(translation)

"Midnight, Christians, it is the solemn hour
when The God-in-Man comes down unto us,
in order to erase original sin
and stay His Father's wrath..."

PROLOGUE

(in which the unseen presence of The Holy Spirit, welcoming them all back to Earth, greets Man in general and, specifically, a Band of Artists/Poets, "Spirit"/St. Francis of Assisi, Lucifer, and God)

I

THE HOLY SPIRIT

Who but I, Holy Spirit, can reside
in the mind (and heart) of every man?
Who can deny the love, then, that may guide

him I shall enter in—or by whose hand?
That love alone is hate's great opposite:
the very core of God's almighty plan

by which compassion even in the pit
turns evil to its alter ego—good.
So, let the world's old balance wheel refit,

with Alpha and Omega understood,
as wickedness with righteousness I fan,
cooling Hell's fevered lust with Heaven's food.

By grace of Christ and spirit, saint and man,
if Satan cannot save his soul, God can.

II

THE HOLY SPIRIT

  Come, Band, near-angels, back to Earth.
There, sweeter Christian purpose awaits you
than men have yet conceived—from His birth.

Rejoice! You're raised again to dust; and who
but God, breathing your first breath as your last,
now returns you, chosen and elect, to

youth and faculties at height of man's vast
intellect and powers? Your charge for life?
Swear, steel, gird up as in your human past

to fight to end, by love alone, that strife
that never ends. Along with reason, charm
with faith and hope and *art* (O subtle knife!).

Seduce poor Lucifer away from harm
to truce with his own battle-weary arm.

III

THE HOLY SPIRIT

And you—teach your lesson, Saint, to man and beast:
that gentle hearts confound complexity,
that arrogance on itself must feast,

lacking the strength of real humility.
Embrace your charge as mentor to this band:
you, best loved of all from fair Italy

whose Tuscan song they'll best understand.
Christ was born his Father's living word
and I their love they would to all remand,

his life the light, the whole world's promise heard
by which men may become God's sons/my doves.
So you're reborn to sing for me, dear bird!

Preach to my sheep I now send forth to wolves
to join in peace, divine and human loves.

IV

THE HOLY SPIRIT

Beware, vain Prince. Mirrors held to light,
depicting truth, also picture you,
and those you're doomed, soon, to fight

may clearly see through your distorted view.
As this world's single, sin-full surrogate
you still must seek your predestined cue:

whether to hold to death, to hate,
or swear that oath all mankind may share in,
through Christian mercy: Heaven's loving fate,

freeing every soul (and yours?) of sin.
To humble self, self-righteous pride may smite;
confession of true longing's hard to win,

but time's last warnings on your wall now write
that love's bright dawning must end hatred's night.

V

THE HOLY SPIRIT

Descend, O God, your quenchless flame on all.
Baptize with me, that they new-Christened be,
these giants who must, to truly heed your call,

join selves to sinner at their Father's knee.
Seal to their hands art's fairest sword
exalting Love incarnate: God/Christ/Me.

Yet they, loved of three, are human, Lord!
Sworn to create their ultimate *chef-d'oeuvre*
they still love their old Earth, of one accord.

They'll pledge their souls to Heaven above,
but love their—and *your*—mortal enemy?
And can *he* return your Christian love?

Who but their shepherd saint, love's epitome,
can bring all back to our Holy Trinity?

ACT ONE

THE ANTICHRIST

(The Last Temptation)

Evening

(in which Lucifer, given human life and one last chance to repent by God, on the very eve of Resurrection, proceeds to tempt the Band of Artists/Poets also restored to early mortality, to join with him in beseeching God to postpone Judgment altogether and prolong Time indefinitely—in exchange for his summoning of their former loves on Earth, and his own sly promise to atone)

1

LUCIFER
(alone)   (*sotto voce*)

Now man comes back to play at mocking Me
 (still dreaming of my other worldly test)
  by wit and clever speeches to prove *he*,

  my rival—*God*—knows him best
and loves him best. *Hah!* Vanity will reign
  as long as I and I will have my jest.

Art-starved man won't see my aim if I feign
 nostalgia for his "genius". So, to praise
  (adorn Hell with Heaven's chosen strain)

  I'll exert most cunning of my ways
   on this eve of final revelation,
   for on that day most telling of all days

 away from him who bargains with his son
  I must win the fruits of resurrection.

(enter Dante *et alii*)

DANTE

Satan! First light our opening eyes discern.
In gilding you, our Lord must have His reason.
Yet I and my immortaled friends still yearn

for brighter welcome to this too brief season,
some heavenly host to counteract our dread
(God forbid our worldly yearning's treason!)

of either fork before tomorrow's fled.
Let me, for this band of artists/poets, bid
you tempt us not by that talent sacred

we, by chisel, brush and pen, on earth propounded:
Goethe, da Vinci, Shakespeare and van Rijn, Milton,
Buonarroti and Alighieri rid

ourselves of you by our acts of last contrition.
(*He smiles!*) No? Then bid us welcome, apparition.

LUCIFER

Obbedisco, signor! And do accept my
warmest greetings, imploring your enlightenment
of Me toward where your buried yearnings lie.

See how my gracious will now burns with pure intent—
pleasing all, upon your mortal sojourn?
Your God bids Me spare no labor to content

you briefly here for he has heard you mourn,
lamenting fleshly death at Heaven's very gate.
Wresting pity, your sad farewell has torn

you loose from him and "love" (and onto Me and "hate"!).
I, too, fear those things I know so little of
And would remain *nel mezzo* our innate

earthly joys. So, let's welcome Earth—above
all else (especially God's commanding love).

MICHELANGELO

As you may wish to welcome Heaven, yet.
Why do you, viewing God's love as affliction,
choose us—God-*lovers*—To abet?

I wonder, too, at His conviction:
false apostates, we—or true apostles—
Which? Will He not pierce this strange constriction

of our faith, shaken from its principles
by this new turn, undreamt of in the grave?
Are we not His—and Art's—invincibles?

Satan, I do marvel—you're so bold and brave!
By casting you in *bas*-relief/plain sight,
perhaps He seeks our candle-flames to save,

lifting our vision gradually from night
on Earth—toward Heaven's brilliant, blinding light.

REMBRANDT

God grant you speak the truth, Buonarroti.
As for me, I'd risk my soul for that light
that, on Earth, constantly challenged me.

To filter it through my once eager sight
on one last splendid canvas ought
to elevate my art to untold height.

Gloat, dark Prince! You I see in dearly bought
but glittering armors fitting to your rank—
vain symbols of our cruelest battle fought.

Still, I'd rather pride and passion sank
than to please you, who my own soul would wrench
from God. For you'd outstrip His legions' flank

although I yielded not one single inch—
and, do-or-die, my fervent flame would quench.

.

SHAKESPEARE

Why do you worry, *mijnheer*? Devils too
will meet comeuppance by this end of time.
Satan—Do you think you'll outwit us? We few

grand masters of the arts of daub and rhyme
have no time for you. But one night we ask
of God to bid *adieu* to Earth sublime.

If immortality were our task
that's won already by our labor's joy.
And though for *ten* millennia you bask—

and all your wiles and blandishments employ—
you do so lack our passion to create,
your frenzy leads you only to destroy.

Are not your speech and actions bent by hate—
like my third Richard who, too, met his fate?

MILTON

God's Word! You all speak well, and you, friend Will.
In truth, we are in God's eternal debt—
that by His grace we are His favorites still

and not Mephisto's willing pawns. And yet
I do covet dispersal of that white
cloud still on my sight—whether but to whet

my appetite for day more than for night,
or not—and I would now (or sooner!) know
if, here on Earth, to free my lingering plight

I'd best look to God or His/our foe.
Let's defer to those whose lucid powers
surpass ours. Sirs—Goethe, Leonardo:

should we, even as our hope of Heaven flowers,
smile or frown on Satan's promised dowers?

GOETHE

Danke schön, Johann. Mein Gott, how brave you
    are to flatter me who usurped Divine
    creation! And all the traits I dared embue

    in *you*, Mephistopheles, devil mine
(and God's), you flaunt, parade here in the flesh:
wit, rage, pride, gall. So, good friends, to entwine

    us he will pledge the world—to enmesh
    us in the one or other, Earth or Hell.
    Famishing for Heaven's fruits so fresh,

    he still foments his ageless plots to jell.
    But even so, from evil we may learn
to choke his gorging with his own death-bell,

    not ours. I urge his offer we not spurn.
    It may spur us a greater good to earn.

LEONARDO

Grazie, milord *Giovan*, but if you'd hold
King Solomon's wisdom, you'd better be
far wiser still than I to mine the gold

inherent in this holy mystery.
You know *my* passion to fuse light with shade,
to unmask the veils which puzzle me

as science into *art* mystically fades.
But for my wonder at each living thing
I would urge we speed him back to Hades,

from Earth. So God from Heaven had to fling
His morning star to wane beneath the skies—
this jealous wretch who thinks himself a king.

Let us hear him out, through his truth or lies;
perhaps we'll then foretell his set or rise.

LUCIFER

    I think, *signori,* you protest too much.
If you fear Me not, why warn Me not to tempt you?
    But hear my plan—you will not find it such

    to touch disquietude. With him who
is your God (or was—on Earth—your god, *art?*)
    I seek your intercession now to woo

    him from his mighty purpose that will start
at barest dawn tomorrow, first to quake
    all those poor souls—both his and mine—apart

    from their deep sleep, believing death would take
them to their joy or woe. So—you alone
must move him—for your "Christian" mercy's sake—

    for you the day of judgment to postpone,
for Me (forse!) to swear then to atone.

DANTE

How cleverly our nemesis now speaks,
piercing to our core—the very name
of Christianity. And what he wreaks

matters not at all if, to our own shame,
we do not practice what we glibly preach:
Mercy. Peace. And love. Each must be our aim.

And yet, how far toward him can we now reach
without leaning too far away from *Him?*
Lacking still some holy one to teach

us what to do, we now approach the rim
(the abyss!) of our last choice for ill
or good. But speak. Your voices are so dim.

Si? Be it so. But oh! Must God fill
us so—with such decided chill?

12

LUCIFER

Eternal thanks, my lords, for your mercy sweet!
You will not have occasion to regret
for I will make your stay here so replete

with those old passions you cannot forget,
burning new for you in breast and eye,
you may proclaim yourselves well in my debt.

And since one deed deserves another, I
swear also to restore to your desires
that fame you thought would never die:

all those heavenly arts conquered through such fires—
sculpting, painting, writing...*poesia;*
All those worldly joys mortal man requires—

Christiane, Beatrice, Vittoria...
Mary, Saskia, Anne...and Monna Lisa.

(enter "Spirit"/St. Francis of Assisi)

SPIRIT
(St. Francis)

Pax et Bonum! God and Jesus Christ
our Lord and Savior are now here with you,
for I, "Spirit" am sent to join your tryst.

Why?—And why so late?—you cry, and I too
share your wonder at Lucifer's embrace.
But as all his seductions you pass through

I am your sword, your trumpet, and your grace.
Who am I else? *Incognito*, I stay
till you see *God*—looking on my face.

Like you, I once was held in such sweet sway
by love of Earth, beyond description's tongue,
that only Heaven-longing could allay

my fear of being sudden stricken dumb
before my praises raised. *Pax Vobiscum!*

LUCIFER

Se permetti, I'll greet you first, "Spirit",
for I too feel the chill your presence brings,
boding Me ill, no doubt, not good. My wit

may disappear now you are here! And things
beyond my realm seep through my brain. But still,
pay Me heed, emissary. Hell sings

my title: Antichrist. So—Heaven will
send you, unknown adversary, against
my magnitude? You know that I would kill

to keep my name—And Me—away from holy taints?
And you—name free.... *Cosi?* Your identity
matters not to Me. Even to their saints

men cast epithets throughout history—
and, in the end, they all come back—to Me.

LUCIFER

Popes on emperors, emperors on popes…
rulers, rulers flay…powers on powers,
my name, Antichrist, 'round their necks like ropes;

religion on religion…yours, mine, ours.
Man, awaiting both the new messiah
and, as well, *his* unnamed assailant's hours,

doesn't heed my constant climbing higher;
waiting for some other, he lets Me—
epitome of evil (true liar!)—

whisper in his ear. How can he be free?
None was, is, shall be mightier than I
at waging war against humanity.

"I am a jealous God…!", your God would cry…
so—only evil, I personify.

SPIRIT
(St. Francis)

Lucifer, we do not care to strip you
naked of your trappings. Your titles all
are yours (at least until the morning dew!).

Your edict does not cast us in a pall;
we have no doubt you are *antichristus.*
He whose high throne you would cause to fall

has named this band of resurrected dust
as His envoys to end this final war
for good that you, evil, still so mistrust.

And since we trust in you neither vice nor
virtue, we wonder how you reconcile
that "Christian mercy" that you ask us for,

when, with such duplicity and obvious guile
you once again entice us with a smile!

MICHELANGELO

Good God! We thank *Him you* are here, Spirit!—
    to bring His succor to our very souls.
    If here to warn us, stop and stay a bit—

though surely Satan's eyes (*twin burning coals!*)
    perform that office for you, and for him.
    Who would dare to doubt his dreadful goals

    when he himself brags of his fatal whim:
    to earn his name—supreme antagonist—
    against all Heaven, Lord and seraphim.

    But let it not be said we missed
    hearing him air his wonders, tricks—harass
    us though he must. So we'll devise the gist

    of our intent. If one night's joy we pass,
    it will not keep us from *God's* dawning Mass.

LUCIFER

How wise you are, dear Michelangelo.
And, since you lean in sympathy toward Me,
take your first choice of temporal joys to sow:

man—woman, angel—devil...what shall be—
your wish—for Me to conjure up? Fear not—
confide Me your inmost desires and see

   them rise to light. By Belial, may I rot
      if I do not succeed in raising them,
   your loves, O Band, upon this very spot.

By God! I learned well, shadowed by *his* hem
   (I think you know why I so fleetly ran),
my wonders to perform, both gay and grim.

   Spirit—if you're here to convert Satan,
   I claim my promised right to subvert man!

MICHELANGELO

    Vittoria I would see—patron, friend,
      fellow poet—cool fire in which I burned.
  (She comes! Here now, at last, my death may end)
(enter Vittoria)

      My marchioness, I kiss your hand; turned
    I see your lips. Chaste bride of Christ, your eyes
      alone still are mine—by forbearance earned.

      God! To see them once again exercise
        dominion over me and all my art—
      my sculptures, and poetry…all our ties.

    Cristo! That *crocifisso,* made, my heart,
for thee, your silence—now—makes for me. *Ma—*
    you embraced *His* body chastely from the start,

and one here knows how much blood that costs. Ah.
    Dante—let her speak! Speak…*per pietà!*

DANTE

Dio, si può, Michelangniolo!
Dare alla luce—poetry's riches:
rimes bejeweled again like stars row on row,

dazzling Hell itself—black as pitch is.
May God so cause His light in us to shine
high enough for our loves in their niches.

Sweet this art (of loving God!) burns—like wine!
Ahimè. It cannot be, on this plane.
Though near, I see they're still beyond that line

we crossed, by God's grace. Lucifer, the bane—
the bone within their throats to strangle speech.
Devil, leave us. You can't even train

your piteous band to cry. No, mend our breach.
Beatrice I would see. So high you reach?

> (following Vittoria, Beatrice and
> her five other companions
> appear, only faintly materialized
> as yet since only their *images*
> are raised by Satan, and not they,
> themselves, by God)

DANTE

You—Here? I wonder—do you see
me, dearest vision—your eyes swift birds
flying beyond death, ever after me?

Oh, God! Can you not speak? How sweet your words
fell on Earth, raining sweeter dreams—chiding
me. *Ma, non importa.* Your smile girds

me for Heaven or Hell. Are you guiding
me again, as before, my way to pave?
Beatrice! By Heaven abiding—

speak but one word and I for you will brave
Hell again—or plagues of Egypt, seven.
But no, our tears seem but to bless the grave.

God, past human strength, our hope must leaven.
Where shall we join our love, Love—in Heaven?

(enter Christiane)

GOETHE

Christiane—*mein liebes Herz—"Gretchen", mine.*
Deep repository of my soul's
delight—love, passion, melancholy's *Wein...*

many a glorious night. "Opposing poles",
they gibed us, and many a verbal war
I fought—defending your more humble goals.

But, like Lucifer, one man may abhor
things which to himself strange and wondrous seem—
which he, unknowing, may be pining for.

So may gold, beneath the Rhine, purely gleam.
Rest quiet, my heart. We need not fret this way.
Your joy-filled eyes are still my dearest dream.

I'll wait yet to hear, some glorious day,
your lips whispering, sweet, *"Io amo te"!*

(enter Mary)

MILTON

Mary? Make haste—bring her to me.
Far too much time we've already lost.
Joined yet split apart too soon, why did we

give up so much and never count the cost?
Love-driven by too many things other
than each other, our love was wild, storm-tossed,

till brought ashore, calmed by one another.
But even as one lifetime is too short
to ever love, enough, one's dear lover—

so one night here, I fear, can but abort
whatever sad remorse my lips might pour
into your ear without your just retort.

I then too will wait, but, imploring more
than is my due, my human hopes will soar.

SHAKESPEARE

Lucifer, show me Anne, if you can. Wife
of my bosom! Now may we cast off gloom?
May we now grant surcease to wedded strife,
(enter Anne)

not strive to create, this eve of doom,
those flickering flames that fanned our fire's content
when I with barren infants filled your womb?

With no more babes to suckle, we have spent
life's brief store of quickening thrust and parry.
Yet I live on, by patrimony lent.

Mourn not, Anne, sons who might've been. Marry!
I am sire of *kings*—grandsire of the same—
English kings…Richard, Lear, and fair Harry!

And these, my progeny, death can never claim.
Remember me, Anne. *England* is my name.

(enter Saskia)

REMBRANDT

My Saskia. I must paint you once again.
So frail you seem—palest living hue.
Shall I hurry before all light may wane,

once more in art to immortalize you?
Must your light inside your grave-clothes hide?
Do I see Bathsheba? Danae, too?

Flora, and Bellona? No, I deride
those earthly aims at love's pre-destiny.
Like Michelangelo, as Christ's bride

I see you only now. And yet, and yet! *See,*
Saskia! *Remember?* Can we still give
and take, with grateful prodigality,

God's worldly gifts? Perhaps He will forgive
my human lust, Earth's dust still to outlive.

(enter Mona Lisa)

LEONARDO

Madonna toscana—Lisa. Dear *God!*
What rapture have we captured in your face?
All I revered in woman; is it odd—

that my own dreamed-of mother bears the trace
of your beauty? And Heaven's royal Queen.
To honor *her*, all talents must abase

their struggle toward perfection's fairest mean.
But if you are not perfect, nor am I,
although within your countenance serene

I glimpse those selves which, with me, seemed to die:
child, wife, lover, friend. Banners high unfurled
could not tell me more; genius cannot lie.

Like Dante's Beatrice, angel-lips curled
in enigmatic smile convey—*the world!*

SPIRIT
(St. Francis)

Right well I see you've kept your word,
   Lucifer—giving to this band their
hearts' desires. May all they've seen and heard

   convince them urgently their faith may bear
repair. Satan! What other have you done—
   than to attempt their thirst and hunger rare

to satisfy with tid-bits lightly won
   and as lightly held when tomorrow's scroll
shall be unrolled? But your campaign's begun

and they would see it through, your promised dole,
if not through you. You know, Band, once he fell;
   now keep your eyes fixed on my higher goal—

   that his ambitions fall again, pell-mell
for I am sent from Heaven; he—from Hell.

SPIRIT
(St. Francis)

And you, Lucifer. You I now invite
to turn back both sight and recollection.
So short a memory! Once you dared incite

the Son of God, spreading your infection
before Him banquet-wise, expecting He
would eat—and be thrown on your protection.

Kingdoms offered—throne/empire/monarchy—
amazed and awed that He resisted such.
Remember your (and Milton's) desert plea

when, persuading not, you then dared much
more than insult: inviting Him to kiss the sod
beneath your feet? But He cast off your clutch.

Turning to this Band, failing Jesus's nod,
you think to tempt them now, and through them—*God?*

LUCIFER

"Gratitude", he cried! when he—*he* declined
all I had to offer—no, all but one.
I did not offer *Me*, although he whined

that he alone is God's own, only son.
If I gave way that's not to say...gave up,
for winning the game yet shall be my fun

and, granting God his due, I'm no pup
lightly to unleash. Am I not still free
to roam the citadel before his cup

of sacrifice I price? He—enemy
of ancient days...Jesus Christ...bloody host...
son!—is but one of holy persons three.

Stay with Me, Band. My wonders you shall toast
as, indeed, I tempt: Father and "Holy Ghost".

DANTE

And so you think to begin with us. Eh,
Lucifer? *Va ben.* See you try your best—
or worst; what that may be, we'll see. *Beh,*

who knows—since He's decreed you be our guest
this restless night perhaps you may relieve
our grief—as we struggle with God's test

of *Love* as well as "love". I can't believe
He will withhold either from us. Our hope
of endless bliss, in Heaven to receive,

sustained our deepest dreams the tomb to cope.
Take care not to relieve us of true goals
while we in Earth's last limbo seem to grope

for sustenance to feed our famished souls.
Lead on, Lucifer—sparing us your tolls.

(exeunt the Band's *Amours*)

ACT TWO

THE ARMAGEDDON

(The Final Battle)

The Dead of Night

(in which the Band, pretending to acquiesce to Lucifer's tempting demands that they remain with him on Earth for the sake of their poetry and art, to which they are indeed, now as ever, powerfully, nostalgically drawn, attempt to persuade him, through that very art—which they encourage him now to recite and to evoke—to accompany them to Heaven)

LUCIFER

    Observe, Spirit, your charges' ardent zeal
        for *God!* So eager are they to be brought to lust,
    that barely fade their whores (who seemed so real!)

before they loudly cry—because they think they must?
        Enough! I'm wearied of human foreplay.
        "On!", you say, Alighieri? *Si!* I'll entrust

    your pleasure (and my pain) to vain array—
        self-tributes men, and gods, have always craved:
"good works"! Not mine, Band (that will be the day)—

but yours. Spirit, for the present, your name's waived.
        I wonder who you are but, if you be
        able, answer this (since I'm to be "saved"):

        your "Spirit, *Holy*"—who, or what, is he...
        that men believe in? What is he to Me?

SPIRIT
(St. Francis)

Do not despise these beings split as one
between my Heaven, your Hell. Human they
appear and you, too, wear new skin, Satan.

Look kindly on their foibles, fancies, fey
ways...you too are mortal now, Lucifer!
God does not require man to lay away

humanness for Heaven—till he, as it were,
yearns (more than anything/anywhere on Earth)
to be *there*, to give up life's blood, and stir

it with the saints'. Do not waste your idle mirth
hinting for my name, mocking me in whim,
as *Holy Spirit*: I do not have *His* worth.

Do not so blaspheme; your new star, too, may dim.
Still and all, he who sees me *may* see Him.

DANTE

Restrain your mania to protect mankind,
Spirit, from him whose fate for nobler blood
is tortuous but strong. I think we'll find,

since God now binds him to us in Earth's mud,
we'll co-exist—whether or not we care
to learn each other's ways all in a flood!

If he ignores our rules then we must dare
to play by his—*sans* all honor, except one:
to warn him what we will! He warned us fair—

if not with words, with intent barring none.
One passion—temptation—is his only game;
but this one last time, shall we be undone?

Though we are seven, the "Trinity" we claim
against that one who swears "Legion" is his name.

LUCIFER

Hah! For one whose love of Earth so defies
"description's tongue", Spirit, you suffer no
breathlessness—for extolling Heaven's lies!

Still, you haven't answered yet, and so
I ask again: just who, and where, is he?
You ask Me to believe more than I know—

or see? I don't believe half I do see!
I see no holy "Ghost", priestly or profane;
if he's in you, or *you*, Dante (never Me!),

I'll tempt two-in-one! This I warn again.
But come, artists/poets! Drink to our good fight.
You choose your swords, I'll chose mine. Boredom's pain

is more than brain can bear—do admit I'm right.
Spirit sets Me ill—such sweetness...such light.

MICHELANGELO

God—knowing we are weak, only seeming strong,
 why must Thou heap this crushing task upon us?
Why must our hearts store up our treasures so long?

 Our marbles have crumbled, our bronzes rust.
  What is Thy purpose, our genius to renew?
 Our paint weeps rivulets, our words breathe dust.

  If we could but know Thy good would ensue.
 But—to tempt us back to Earth...to work, to stay...
 then, doubtless, to be drawn into Hell's dark view...

   This—his purpose we know well: to betray
   to that second death that which was our life.
   Dante, I know—God!—I share your dismay.

    But...if *art* could sweeten that bitter strife
      that, with God and devil, is ever rife.

LUCIFER

Ecco! Thus Tuscan "genius" and rare wit
artlessly declare God's most artful war!
Spirit, *you* may now flit away; quit

hovering about; go plead with God—or
say no to judgment day. Why vacillate?
Why not admit you have no stomach for

Heaven—yet? You know I'll reciprocate
such courtesy. After all, your desires,
dear Band: to recreate old art/create

the new—new monuments to passion's fires,
God's or man's, are as plain as mine to see.
And if to thrust old talent to new spires

I must expel *him* from your minds, as he
once banished Me—is this too high a fee?

MICHELANGELO

It's not so strange you know our worldly woes
and weak points, Satan—since you bestow them.
Still, high achievements rise from those same throes

and achings of desire devils stay stern
from them, not God: fever, so burning bright—
alive we die and, dying, still live. Dim

our hopes to transcend flesh while you incite
us to new heights of passion—for our *art*.
But wait. Do you dare, human now, recite

those mortal words which light us—soul, mind, heart,
to immortality?...evoke, we trust,
our real lust?...risk being torn apart

by true art? I do not. Yet if I must...
Dear God! I pray Christ may watch over us.

LUCIFER
(aside)

(These prating mortals ramble so, I swear
preaching is their gift, not art. And so pat
their sermons I must sift through—to lay bare

what they really mean. We'll play tit-for-tat.)
Certo, Michelangelo. I'll spit
out that "art" you, painter/poets, have spat

on an adulating world, sucking dry your tit:
self-righteousness, self-honor and self-love.
Deny it, Band—if you can. Say—is it

real, or pseudo—your zeal for God above?
Silenzio, Toscani. Save your song.
Goethe, *erst:* his "Devil" fits Me like a glove.

Oh, I'll prove my charge as we move along.
Just try—if you care (dare) to prove Me wrong.

GOETHE

Oh, it's real, dear Mephistopheles.
As you'll be but too happy to agree—
before we write *finis*. Now, if you please

assume your place on stage. As for me—
Faust pleases me. What else? I yearn
to hear God's words, through mine, set free.

Agreed, Devil? You give me quite a turn,
you know. Each time I hear your gibes, your quips
judging His creation, man, I discern

you, Satan, would dance upon our crypts
unjudged, forever! But there, never mind.
Gott im Himmel now consecrate your lips—

and mine—to His great purpose till we find
that *dénouement* toward which our prologues wind.

LUCIFER
(after reciting Goethe's entire *Faust* Prologue)

Gott! Why do you weep so, *Herr Professor*?
To mime your rhyme means nothing more to Me
than acting a part I neither mean nor

agree. Such sentimental claptrap! See
you vomit up no more charitable lies
that so besmirch my real identity.

As God says: Man errs, even as he tries.
"Gleam of heavenly light...reason"...? *Quel ennui.*
Passion, not reason, governs human cries.

But true—Me, he grants *carte blanche* to be free.
For that, even to Christ, some thanks I'd disburse,
though God, no kindly words, but yours, pays Me.

Now I fear your kindliness may yet prove my curse,
Am *I* to be crucified?—*on Art...and Verse?*

GOETHE

In a word, yes, Satan—*Dei gratia.*
Now leave me, for Christ's sake, to contemplate
that which our Tuscans call *poesia*...

that which I call life—my work and my fate,
my art. My *Faust!* What more can I now do?
From my soul I cry: is Heaven so great

that I shall love it more than I love you?
Is not art, once given, at long last, birth—
in itself enough? Should this not be true?

The more fool I! Where else but on this Earth
strives man to celebrate his peers by that ray
of wisdom, passion, *joy* that pits their worth

against his own? Thus Shakespeare...Milton...Dante—
by their genius—brought forth my passion-play.

GOETHE

My love for God, you ask—is it real? Ah!
How real it really is I dare not say.
Ich bin my poem/my poem *bin ich! Nicht wahr?*

The play must speak for me, not I the play!
Not even you, Lucifer, can negate—
by scoffing/laughter/insults that portray

denial—that *deep meaning* words that grate
upon your stony heart cleave to your soul.
Thus must God's word stand revealed, soon or late.

O sweet philosophy—and sweeter goal:
that man from grievous sin may still be passed
to Heaven's glory—know himself made whole

with God. *Ich dien* and so shall you, at last.
Till then, Satan—*ohne Hast, ohne Rast.*

REMBRANDT

Willingly or not, Satan, if I'm right,
you once cajoled God's ear—if not His crown.
When not so far removed from Heaven's light,

you sang, yourself, a lighter tune, O clown.
As Goethe proves, you must have some regrets
at leaving God with lesser angels 'round.

Now learn your human nature, which abets
essential evil to potential good.
And so to pay our intercession's debts

further, revitalize my art. I would
see my "Artist and his Wife", Lucifer...
                    (the painting materializes)
Oh, *Saskia!*—*darling* mine—would that I could

dance you upon my knee! Ah, there we were!—
so carefree, as if time lasts forever.

LUCIFER

Bravo! Rembrandt—but for you, art's a yawn.
I'll crack my jaws over those boring themes
Goethe *et alii* pontificate on.

But you, *mon cher ami*, love life, not dreams
of new-risen flesh and "Life" yet to come.
Only you, of the Band, show "wisdom's gleams"—

good wine...good wife...good life, my dear *bonhomme!*
Reclaim, *je vous prie*, your *vie de bohème*.
Smile, van Rijn! Why on Earth are you so glum?

Do you, then, pine to refine this rare gem
that I, of all your art, dub your crown jewel?
Why not decide to stay gay, not grim?

We'll be allies in art's most costly duel.
Choose Heaven over Earth? Be not so cruel!

REMBRANDT

But why do you not choose Heaven, Satan—
you who, more than we, know that it exists?
Does it not wring your heart—what you have done,

what you have given up for Hell's emptiness?
Have you no conscience, no regrets, even one—
you, who dared challenge *God* and raise your fists?

Paradise! To think—you have looked upon
God Himself, and then turned your back on Him.
God in Heaven! First the Father, then the Son;

now the Spirit, who would fill you to the brim.
Even in my art you refuse to see
"love" and sensual pleasure but skim the rim

of our need to love—to drink—divinity,
to slake the deep thirst of our humanity.

REMBRANDT

In good time—my "Prodigal" I'll command.
First, Lucifer, my "Jakob" you must meet.
              (his painting, Jacob Wrestles
                with the Angel, appears)
See? Look—how gentle that all-embracing hand

that, breaking, still blesses the savage heart's beat.
Perceive: the grieved yet compassionate glance
He bends on His prince, to serve so sweet.

That servant is you—whose one last chance
to greet Him face to face and stand preserved
is fading, Satan, fading. Still He grants

your birthright's bright return—if well deserved.
Before saying no, Satan, weigh each thought.
Look now upon my Prodigal, all unnerved,
              (his painting, The Prodigal
                Son, is evoked)
scarce deserving hope, so near and far he sought.
Can you believe what we, in art, have wrought?

LUCIFER

"Et tu, Brute?" Have I, then, no surcease
from pious platitudes and lessons ill-taught?
Rave on. Moralize—let your lies increase.

They'll find no mark in Me; I won't be caught.
What "we" have wrought? Indeed! To listen, one thinks
you conceived creation, not *he*. So fraught,

complacently, your highest ideal shrinks.
You low-rate Me to elevate yourselves.
That's your game, eh?—to praise God till he blinks,

with your fine arts the probe my grossness delves?
Even to your God you show selfish pride.
Who's more in need of hope—your godly selves

(*Christian* hypocrites, I can't abide)
or Me, tempted true, wrestling *him* inside?

LUCIFER

Ah, I do grasp the gist of your intent,
Michelangelo. Stupid Me, not to see
you meant to do Me in as you were sent

from the beginning. Now I'll, with my usual glee,
at English "argument", quote Milton's lies;
before he seeks my vote on his poetry!

Goethe and Rembrandt made good their tries
at softening Me, to face again their Christ.
I know them too well to believe them wise

to promise hope (where none exists) so overpriced.
They forget I'm ages old, past foolish youth—
to believe the fairy tales they have spliced.

(I hope I don't forget wrong from right—how uncouth!
If I'm not *en garde*, I'll learn to like this "truth".)

> (he recites, seemingly at random,
> several out-of-sequence excerpts
> from *Paradise Regained*)

MILTON

To know just why you chose those words to quote,
    Satan, is as clear to me as is this day.
  Shall I expound? You do not quote by rote—

  like it or not, you do mean what you say.
  Though you deny His impact with your mind,
    your heart and soul can't hold Him at bay.

    Transpose art as you will, front behind
  the end—so would you turn back, at all cost.
    Can it be—not to find but to rewind

  time is your fate?...to regain what was lost?
You can, Satan! Why in Hell, should you mope?
  Your thoughts, like my words, are crisscrossed.

  Can't you reach out for Jesus's gentle rope,
and so advance through scorn, and doubt, to hope?

MILTON

Listen, Satan, to my/your prophetic words just
uttered. Would you have the Christ, were he so
easy to win? He if anyone, you can trust;

He, more than we, is more friend than foe.
As you do not give up, neither does He
and He'll not rest till you've renounced Hell below.

Begin, then. Remember. We have the key
to unlock your frozen heart and let Him in.
Once you were tempted—to His shelter, flee,

and now, how dare you—His patience to run thin?
God Himself, alone, knows where each road ends;
only through Him can you hope to win from sin.

His is the way—even for you it bends:
"So fares it when falsehood with truth contends."

LEONARDO

All our works of art reflect but a trace
of beauty, truly, from their Christian source.
From one, alone, of mine—His holy face

shines forth such radiance, such forgiving force,
    to hearten even you, Lucifer:
Ultima Cena. Deny Him till you're hoarse,
        (his painting, The Last Supper, appears)

there He awaits, patiently, Passover
of your last human hope to cross His breast.
Good men, too, fall prey—Peter was no cur.

But Pilate, Judas, Satan—may find rest...
may receive His cup, brimming love to drain...
may believe His covenant, and be blessed.

So, with kiss or curse, betray Him not again,
and pray God shall not—for you—have died in vain.

LEONARDO

One of you will betray me, said the Christ,
knowing, in His heart of hearts, what must be.
Whether for the lowest, or the highest—

His love, alone, equals God's mercy.
Before Him all are humble—even I,
before His glance I cower unworthily;

my artist's brush may never lift His eye.
You, Satan, stealing nearer, may yet find,
unless you cause yourself too soon to die,

what gleams, beneath His gaze, for humankind.
Compassion or contempt—one is your due.
Salvation? Damnation? Are you resigned?

(As bread and wine transfigure man, *Gesù,*
may not even *he* eat, drink, live—through You?)

LUCIFER

If we had more time, *Ser* Leonardo,
I might indulge your flattery.
Whether you speak for *him*, I don't know

or care. Should we (note our royal "we")
swear false "hope" just to flatter him? Not yet.
My other selves and I must stay free,

must steer clear of surety for all debt—
to eager zealots out to save our "soul".
So you too, Master John, conspire to beget

art so pure to lure my iron heart to gold?
Fools! I would not have your Christ, by any key.
I?—give up all Hell, just because I'm told?

I shall not serve; I shall not bend a knee.
Save yourselves, savants. I'll look out for Me.

LUCIFER

Ah, Dante! *Caro*. Must you, too, believe
this is my last chance to bow to your king?
Consider, instead, all that you may leave

buried here on Earth once his trumpets ring.
Think, Dante, think. If you take pen in hand—
nothing is mightier: sword...angel's wing—

the Band will follow. Make them understand
the art you'll create—for God, if you must;
but for yourselves, just hear what I've planned:

time—to climb again or delve the Earth's crust...
to surpass the past. What but art endures?
Now, turn and turn about—am I not just?

Ascolta, Dante. Time itself adjures.
Speak. What shall Satan yield? The field is yours.

DANTE

Si. Io—poet whose words lie moribund,
crushed, under the gravestones of centuries,
hearing them sudden raised and fairly sunned,

even by you—Dark Prince and Sire of Lies—
fall drunk for such ambrosial dew. Paeans of praise,
reclaiming fame's wreathèd brow with glad cries.

Can Charon's farewell herald more joyful daze?
Poeta pazzo! Dio! Recitativo?
Recite: your and Vanni Fucci's hellish ways.

Preserve, by all means, your alter ego,
or we may forget we know who serves us ill.
Ma avanti, Satan, hurry. I too must know—

can my beloved poem my passions still thrill?
Can my own *Comedy* my heart still fill?

(Lucifer quotes Cantos 25 and 26,
in toto, from *The Inferno*)

LUCIFER

There. *Lei piace*, Dante? Are you pleased—
    to admire poetry that so defies
your death and its own? Then I, too, am seized

    with admiration for your art...deep sighs
    heave from my breast (nostalgia for *my* art!).
As for my art, wickedness, whose grand prize

no peer wins (this world for the next), the heart
of Hell (Myself) alone spawns each heartless
    sin that perpetrates evil, tears men apart

    to burn through eternity. Now confess
    how *art* dares hope obliterate the glee
    sinners take to murder, rape, maim. Unless

    Heaven hopes to steal Hell's supremacy,
    what has mere thievery to do with Me?

LUCIFER

And, *amico mio,* Dante—*dica Me*:
If the Almighty will not countenance hate
(namely, Me), why does he *love* (his son) purvey

to mankind when, assuredly, it's too late?
It's a paradox, to Me, why he,
knowing man to be careless of his fate,

makes life on Earth so dear a luxury
that man, bound for Heaven, goes by way of Hell.
Your sinners, once in Hell, it seems to Me,

scorning instead of mourning Heaven, passing well,
rage for loss of Earth. Thus their spiteful ways,
like our master thief's, mock both God and judgment's knell.

Whose fault but God's—that man for days on days,
profligate with time, unrepentant stays?

DANTE

Why, we too might cry, does God permit you,
evil, so to flourish? *Credimi*—He
has His reasons, whether many or few.

But of that we'll speak anew *più tardi*.
As to whether I believe this may well
be your last chance for good, as ours: Ah, *sì*.

Then why must my heart on your temptations dwell?
Silence, to poets, is death...agony
beyond all imagining—outside of Hell.

I'd give all (but my soul) once more to be
secure on this Earth in the rebirth of art.
Satan, you've awakened us and our artistry,

and God in Heaven knows, angel without heart,
as friend or foe you're tearing us apart.

DANTE

Can it be God's will—humanizing you,
causing you to feel love as well as hate,
will cause this Band to take a kinder view?

Is *Love your enemy!* our mortal fate?
Oh, most arduous task...oh, fearsome song to sing.
Embrace "Hell" himself?—a rare human trait,

for all we love the gifts he swears to bring....
But—to love this giver more than his gift.
Ah! There's a present fit to bring our King.

Satan, do you dare help art heal our rift,
and admit your own temptation to our goals?
The moral of my thieves is easy to shift:

Satan, beware of stealing Christian souls—
unless you'd die to try our Christian roles.

LUCIFER
(aside)

(Oh, *God!* To whom else can I cry but *God?*
In my own agony of human doubt,
what higher solace soothes me on this sod?

Myself? Bah! With all others here about
assured of my "soul", how can I steal time
to re-assure me? They mustn't find me out—

this fanatic band—mustn't see that I'm
besotted by their art—frantic to seek
the source of that joy they employ in rhyme

and lime. They'll laugh if *I* too sudden speak
of love for their Christ they idolize so.
God!—why, of a sudden, am I so weak?

Has mortality struck its mortal blow?...)
Sono pronto, O Michelangelo.

MICHELANGELO

Anch'io, Devil, Satan—"Tomaso".
Never since Thomas bared *His* wounded side
has the naked truth, most revealing art, so

awesomely indulged arrogance and pride.
Still you doubt, skeptic?...mock divinity...
swear and desecrate...scoffingly deride

our own life's blood?—our Christianity!
We have staked our souls—impassioned to win
dream from reality, mad to set free

our fiery visions of God's love for men—
on destiny, and genius. Still I bring
you pity, whose eyes are glazed by sin.

If it is art, our idol and our king,
God knows it's to Him our praises sing.

MICHELANGELO

Guarda, Satan. Now look upon my art.

then doubt no more what heart and eye have seen.

It is my *Pietà.* Why do you start?
                 (the sculpture—*Madonna
                  della febbre*—is revealed)

Look where you're going, not where you've been.

Evil had it's purpose—to bring Him low,

that man, by His sacrifice, might be clean.

Mater doloroso—such tender glow!

With Child/Man/Son of God mortal on her knee;

still chaste, innocent, pure as virgin snow...

pity and piety, divine mystery—

faith unriven by nails that pierced His flesh.

Ah, Lucifer. If love yields such ecstasy,

might hate, yielding so—to His Cross and *Crèche*—

win resurrection, and be born afresh?

LUCIFER

No! I'm too weary (frightened!) to look.
You artists/poets would make a devil saint!
It's too much. Have pity! Why must you rook

Me to exacerbate my guilty taint?
I don't believe you—there is no hope
for Me. *Basta,* Christians, or I shall faint.

Oh! How my head reels—addled by the scope
of your queer faith that *I* could ever change.
Leave Me alone! I was learning to cope

with loneliness and exile, in my range.
I don't believe you...but still...my heart quails.
I, who caused His death, His breath to feel? Strange!

I—believe in *Him? No!* My pity fails.
I haven't seen His wounds—or felt the nails.

SHAKESPEARE

"Enough!"—insatiate Satan? Heaven's foe,
   Satan, satiate? *Hell*—bored with villainy?
   If so—where then shall all my villains go?

Good *God,* but it is hard for man—for *me*—
   to cry farewell to all on Earth we love,
   passing Heaven's love, so passionately.

Even my own plays, Christian-born, by Jove,
   seem as pagan, as war-torn, as your Hell!
   And yet—my players, if play-acting, strove

   over evil. If I served art too well—
with warring England's noblest battle cries—
it was, *pour Dieu et mon Droit,* but to quell

Godless emnity! So now my art will rise
as Satan tries King Henry Fifth's disguise.

> (Lucifer declaims the battle
> speeches from Act III,
> Scene 1, and Act IV, Scene 3,
> of *Henry the Fifth*)

SHAKESPEARE

God's blood, you mock/unfrock me well, Devil!
How that pure English flood undams my lust—
   for *England!* How poets love to revel

  in their own native tongues! If back to dust
    I go, I must bare my own naked truth:
  how bitter—yet how sweet—now to entrust

the secret of my grave, heart, age and youth
   to you, newly-human Satan: that we—
men—are devilish too! I swear, to my ruth,

  that England—her language, art, royalty—
    I love with too fair loyalty. Do you,
    new-mortal Lucifer, begin to see...

why I (King Richard now—my poet's view)
so love *English*: so tender...tough...and true...?

                     (Lucifer enacts Act I, Scenes
                     1 and 2, and Act V, Scene 3,
                     from *Richard the Third*)

SHAKESPEARE

Well said, dread Lucifer! What awesome sum
of wisdom meant for all, God's Word can tell
between poets' words, if His intent we plumb.

Now you, as we, receive His mortal spell.
King Richard, hating God, himself, and man,
unwilling hears the fated wedding bell:

dreaded inward Armageddon which can
join God, in man, to devil—till one dies!
Thus is born man's conscience, self-hate to fan,

self-love to ban—except through God's own eyes.
Unless we seek, past wisdom, love's great force
to prise us from the jaws of guilt's sharp vise,

we are doomed to mount, conscience to unhorse
us from our Hell-bent course...*sans* true remorse.

LUCIFER

Where indeed shall Satan go? I don't know!
As wretched sinners writhed in my web before,
you, artists/poets who'll never let Me go,

seal my *coup de grâce sans* one drop of gore.
As He followed John, to be baptized
by him who knew His worth to its burning core,

so I'm followed by one whom He prized—
one by whom my own death blow may be dealt,
though you, Band and Bard, so battle-scarred, sized

my pyre well. What fires my heart to melt:
two English...two Teutons...three from Tuscany!
By whose earthly hand shall they say I knelt?

Does it really matter? There's no land for Me—
Heaven-barred and sick of Hell. *Quelle ironie.*

68

LUCIFER

Will you now hear, Shakespeare, my fateful choice?
Your Wolsey's "Henry Eighth", who serves Me well
and so honors you—this, my final voice.

Can man confess more penitent farewell?
A long farewell, as well, to you, "sweet Prince"—
poet of all England, the world's poem to tell.

English...German...Hollander, all soon hence—
Tuscans: all Heaven-bound—friends, mentors, guides.
This world, nor I, shall know such eminence

again. Spirit! Is it you who over-rides
my will so my temptation boomerangs?
Who *are* you from whom my every instinct hides?

Oh, how I suffer conscience's bitter pangs
and pay the price that guilt at Me harrangues.

(he delivers Wolsey's Farewell
from Act III, Scene 2,
from *Henry the Eighth*)

ST. FRANCIS
(Spirit)

Must you see to believe, Lucifer—that you
are human now as Christ was human then?
See, then! His brand of love shall pierce you, too:
                (he raises his palms in blessing,
                  revealing the stigmata—and his
                  own unmistakable identity)
His anguish and His joy—to vanquish sin.
It is I, Assisi—Earth's lowly saint—
sent to guide home His beloved, sheepish men,

conjoined at last in peace with love's last constraint
within ourselves—our own humanity:
dear beast we cannot flee! But first please paint

with words, for me my prayer—my humble plea.
See. Lucifer—God will not turn you free.
Turn back to Him and you shall baptized be

In nomine Patris et filii
et (dear Brother Wolf) *Spiritus Sancti.*

LUCIFER

Bernardone, I see you would betroth—
by sweeping all my doubts (and sins?) away—
me to God by your soft words, before the oath.

Strangely, I am disposed, through you, to say
"...*let me sow love*..." Can I now believe?
And bring myself to my own judgment day?

Can this importuning Band, who still so grieve
for their sweet Earth, turn Me back whence I came?
Why must I so yearn, yet spurn, to retrieve

Heaven, where from I tempted them—to my shame.
St. Francis! Swear—grant me this one coup:
shall I, before I die, dare cry *His* name?

To you, perhaps...of all men who've loved Earth, you...
whose love for God in Heaven touches Satan, too...

> (he recites Francis's "prayer" and
> then, sinking to his knees,
> falls insensate to the ground)

ST. FRANCIS

Fear not, Lucifer. Dreams, not death, fare you well.
When I return from Heaven I shall bear
light—to brighten even the nightmares of Hell...

life—to heighten even your deep despair.
And if my seeming harshness gave you pause
to doubt Christ Lord's re-descent to Hell where,

drowning in the miasma of your flaws,
you yet sought some sure sign that Heaven cares,
it was to better serve your mortal cause

by virtue of this Band's immortal snares—
visions of Christian art, love, charity—
freeing Satan's passion to rejoin God's heirs.

Soon, Lucifer, from wildest fantasy,
you'll waken to your star's re-ascendancy.

DANTE

Poor beast! He sleeps, deeply, fearing we
forsake God, follow him, forswear *our* judgment day!
Thus is our tempter tempted, happily

unaware that even yet he shall have his way,
while guilt piles on guilt, most dreaded consequence
of allegiance lightly held, once sworn to obey...

of good seduced to evil, beyond all sense...
of love, feared lost, desired more passionately.
Poor sinner! He sleeps, in blessed innocence,

dreaming he is still God's grievous enemy,
swearing true atonement in his heart.
Francis! Is this, then, our human legacy:

sympathy for sin, Heaven's hope to Hell impart—
and love...mankind's most sacred work of art?

> (Francis, smiling, nods affirmatively,
> raises his hand again in benediction
> over them all, and departs)

ACT THREE

THE APOCALYPSE

(The Ultimate Choice)

Dawn

(in which St. Francis returns, bringing Lucifer and the Band face to face with Jesus Christ and into the presence of God, to learn at last the nature of Divine retribution and the extent of Divine mercy— for every man)

ST. FRANCIS
(reappearing)

Arise, O Band! I come, and, after, He—
The *Christ*, whose Second Coming is foretold.
in sacred parable and sainted prophecy.

If faith, or human works, could make man whole,
and Lucifer, your art-struck protégé,
then you alone might ease his restive soul

by virtue raised up to this judgment day,
venturing the very brink of Hell and back,
genius sacrosanct—passion's purest ray.

But even you, Band, sense your awesome lack
and stand transfixed before *God's* passion hurled
from Heaven into men's hearts, sealing intact

faith *and* good works: His grace divine entwirled.
Behold—the Lamb of God...Light of this World!

(enter, The Lord Jesus Christ)

JESUS CHRIST

Dear Saint. My Francis. Where do you belong?
Head above the clouds...feet upon this loam...
You, troubadour, whose life is one sweet song

to God in Heaven, have herded my sheep home:
Heaven to Earth and Hell and back—God's grand tour;
how their human souls, and my spirit, roam!

You have fed my sheep, given to the poor,
quenched their mortal thirst with immortality,
fulfilling man with love—hatred's sole cure—

from my earthly font...Christianity.
Not only would you set my starved lambs free
to graze from worldly folds nearer heavenly,

but the wolf as well—hear his hungry plea?
He and your flock belong—with you—in me.

JESUS CHRIST

Beloved Band, I see how you love me. Do
you not yet see my Father's love? Look
how He loves me...and see how *I* love you.

Rejoice—your names are written in my book.
As I love you, you love one another;
but what of Lucifer who need but crook

bewitching smiles to wile you by, demur
as you will? Satan's beguilements *I* have known:
to spill the cup of life. Do you concur

that man's human frailty still must be honed
into divine perfection? I am the tree,
the fruit, the bread and wine of life. You, my own,

if you would commune with me (can you yet see?)—
if you would be perfect—love *him*...for me.

JESUS CHRIST

Now is your judgment, O Prince of this world.
How shall I judge you...sore in need of me?
Your brow is troubled; are your dreams so whirled

between Heaven and Earth? Is Hell such agony
that Satan would give up, begin the climb:
from the depths to the height of man's nobility?

Or will you, still, perpetuate your crime:
against his better wit, committing man to Earth—
to his frantic search, racing against time,

for happiness not found in *this* world's wide girth.
Tell me what you've learned from humanity—
yours and the Band's as well—the soul's worldly berth.

Lucifer. Come forth. Do not hide from me.
Do you think your soul shall be given free?

(Lucifer stirs and reluctantly awakens)

LUCIFER

Not *Christ!* Francesco, let me look on you.
I dare not smile at *Him*, or call His name.
Yet in your blazing gaze, through my crazed view,

He...smiles on me! How dare you look the same?
I wake but to scoff, doubting—everything,
sure I've had my jest, sure I've won the game.

So this can't be real...can't be happening!
Surely I still dream—that Hell nightmares deal.
How else believe *He* is all forgiving,

God merciful, the Band still full of zeal?
Lucifer to give birth?—his soul's nativity?
Oh, to believe their powerful appeal—

lighting me to Heaven via mortality.
But I swear I dare not. *He* is reality.

JESUS CHRIST

Devil, God made you human to the hilt,
Now you receive man's double-bladed trait:
human emotion. Grief over your guilt...

hope above despair...love far higher than hate.
I, too, wrestled God—on that bitter-sweet road
man undertakes to transubstantiate

self into spirit. But whatever his code,
whatever his creed, mankind must believe
the brightest lodestars truly reflect the lode.

Thus by the glow of my saint you perceive,
and by man's flaming sword of artistry:
images of my love they together weave.

Believe, never doubt, the power of humanity
to light all human souls back to divinity.

LUCIFER

How can I not fear Thee, Son of the living Lord?
Have I forgot Thou spurned me in the wild?
And how avoid lamenting man's adored

Christ, crucified, whose death, crime most reviled,
thy genius-Band has charged to my account—
they, whose stubborn faith so shrewdly styled

that *pietà* no lesser art could mount
in Satan's icy heart. But now I see
Thee, risen, living—from whose glorious fount

all blessings flow...am I to believe...toward me?
What vengeance shall Thy judgment then accord?
Compassion—for the Devil! Can it be?

Thy forgiveness cuts deeper than a sword.
Can Thou, from this Devil, devils cast, Lord?

JESUS CHRIST

Now is my Father's word in your heart sown—
by man's sharpest swords into ploughshares turned.
Now that the word on fertile ground is thrown,

cast your own evil out. Judgment you have earned
and judgment shall receive. But why remit
all hope? Is it so painfully learned

that God is prepared not only to fit
punishment to your crimes but to your amends?
Spent at last by sin, *do* you repent of it?

Shepherds pursue their sheep where Hell itself sends;
I, seeming cold, spoke unforgivingly
to plant that longing only Heaven ends.

Lucifer, Lucifer! Do you yet see—
the love that flowers in you for me?

JESUS CHRIST

While Lucifer death-struggles against peace,
take off God's armor and think on these things—
those inhumanities to man that cease

as love, not war, gives understanding wings.
Remembering man's perverse propensity—
desire for that he thinks fate takes, not brings—

you, Band, have slain well his complacency.
The closer time unending nears his gain,
he dreams and hopes and yearns, *more* passionately,

for that he secretly fears lost. He'll remain
on Earth (with you beside him to proceed
to Hell), but what he most longs to re-obtain

is Heaven! Till your decision *his* has freed,
remember—he will follow where you lead.

LUCIFER

Oh Lord!—I crave indulgence that I speak
before this favored Band whom Thou address.
The inner working of their minds, like Greek—

no, Babel!—baffle me. Before I redress
my wrongs, I would know truly how they think
and if for God—or Devil—they profess.

Can such *Earth*-loving men make Hell extinct,
or turn me from my first, accursèd choice—
this worldly Band who drive me to the brink

of my ultimate and last, final choice?
Proud Band...gentle saint—both preach humility.
Sometimes I think I hear it in each voice!

Must I merely dream they'll give up art for Thee?
Do I dare to hope they'll give up Earth...for me?

DANTE

From those supernal joys that rule the rod
over man: love of life, Earth, land, woman, art...
can't you understand the love we bear *God*

Eternal is, *soprattutto*, a thing apart?
Greedy, we are—for every sweet repast,
human, *si!* But, still, impassioned to impart

life after death. You, Lucifer, stood fast
to rule *me* with—if anything on Earth—
my poetry. This is not to say at last

we are not tempted. We would fill our dearth,
know passion is not spent—in life...faith...art.
But as He ransomed us, back to His hearth,

we must ransom you—denying our heart
what we love most, except our faith: our art.

ST. FRANCIS

Ah, si, è vero, Dante, *cher confrère,*
 that man is never more violently torn
  than by those things aspired to, not to err,

and those he clings to, by his manner born.
 None more than we—none more so than I—see:
  even saints, before worldliness is shorn,

are, first, men. God's happiest faculty,
 creating for mankind a paradise,
  made poets...painters...saints (O Italy!)

that man might see, on Earth, Heaven through our eyes.
 Still, though for Italy *and* France, I sigh,
  it is His *creature* whom I prize.

By my oath, no man loves God more than I—
 yet is more loath...to kiss this world good-bye...

LEONARDO

Grazie, santo mio. Our human task,
to sound at last humanity's retreat,
sounds sweeter from your lips—from that same cask

wherein repose our most sacred, sweet
and inmost selves, our souls—which never lie.
Francis, tell us why, even in our heat

of genius-fire, when passions burned so high,
we refused to see we win what we lose...
possess by giving up...*live* though we die.

Only now we grasp that if we well choose—
Heaven over Earth, Satan can afford
to choose Heaven over Hell! By this ruse

may we merit love from Christ, our dear Lord,
and from Almighty God earn our reward.

REMBRANDT

Leonardo, I share your eagerness
to see God in His Heaven and all right
with the world, and with great joy I confess

my sympathy for him with whom we fight.
My own resurgent urge—to lead that one
who has dwelt in darkness back to the light—

brings to mind my life's most urgent passion:
laboring through art to help man understand
that Light which, dazzling darkness, pales the sun!

So let me hasten to extend my hand,
uplifting his travailing soul before
forgetting I—who worship woman and,

of all things here on Earth, my art adore—
cannot deny I love my God...so much more....

MILTON

Yes, Rembrandt. Now *I* begin to see—
from our acknowledged mission new perceived,
that higher earthly duty calling me.

Though pride, confessing fault, is much aggrieved,
in truth there was some truth to Satan's charge
against our Band though I had not believed

(so eagerly men's consciences enlarge!)
my "Paradise" he could with guilt afflict—
assail my art, as Egypt's queenly barge

sailed into Caesar's heart. How Satan tricked
us all (himself, most of all) by his hungry
human need which we, by Jesus hand-picked,

only now see. Sweet Christ! All our thanks to Thee
that we, so blind so long, at long last see.

SHAKESPEARE

So, gentlemen. At last we face our fate—
    admitting that until we see our God,
we can with neither hand nor heart create

    greater tributes worth hauling in a hod
to Hell, much less to Heaven. How shall we
then make peace with time? To unloose one's cod-

    piece is no answer! I think we agree
God shall reward, all in good time, desire
    for joy on Earth—beyond infinity.

    So let us try once more all to inspire
        Lucifer to create virtue. Shall we
    declare our vilest villains to expire

    so he, renouncing villainy, may be
with us heart and soul through eternity?

GOETHE

Here—of all men tempted by Lucifer
to die for "love"—here...am I. Who *am* I
but my *Faust?* Sensualist, philosopher,

and poet. Sick with love, I cast off my
ties—all but faith! Here, we part good company,
my lifelong friend—belovèd Faust—and I.

Satan has loved Hell, inexplicably.
So is man true to his own worldly mind;
now I, too, must put Earth's love behind me—

help God help Satan his redemption find.
At least he has found wisdom—that "gleam of
heavenly light" that illuminates mankind.

Now, tempted by tempting—hatred back to love,
Satan, shall we not all return above?

MICHELANGELO

Can you still think our god, on Earth, was art?
Must we our talents' purpose still defend:
sweet hope of Heaven—wringing from the heart

our finest works of art...our poetry finely penned?
No, Lucifer. Art is our humble means
to *God*, Almighty—our most exalted end.

Now our worthiness of Him—and yours—leans
upon the altar of His sacrifice.
We enter now into our final scenes.

Satan, give up Hell. Heaven has its price:
His life for mankind...genius for our King...
wealth for poverty... how shall fall your dice?

Will you accept His life, reject death's sting...
admit *you, too, love God*—more than anything?

JESUS CHRIST

Father, O my Father, remove *this* cup from me.
Have I not fulfilled from the beginning,
without end, Thy will—as inexorably

as God-in-man can? As Thou art my king—
divinity—who humanly begot
me, out of love for man, so I now cling

to my human hope Thou require me not
this day—to judge humankind. Forgiveness
is my forte...love, my fever, burning hot.

As man loves man more, shall I love him less?—
and yet expect him to believe I too
forgive my enemy—never to transgress

from my redeeming love? Father, judge them true.
Father, *forgive* them! They know, now, what they do.

(enter, The Lord God)

GOD

Thou art my Son, indeed—in whom I am
well pleased. Never more than now as you stun
this new-born world, my apocalyptic lamb!—

thought vengeful...stern...remote—now seen as one
far nearer to man's heart than Adam's rib.
How superbly true you stay, my beloved Son—

exerting peace on Earth beyond Mary's crib—
to your own human nature, your own divine yen
for love far beyond fair words and gestures glib,

though won by our sinner from Earth's fairest men.
Stay your hand, O Savior. Whether or not
Satan/Lucifer repudiates sin,

you will love him still, deny it one jot.
Love him then. I'll fulfill God's judgment's lot.

GOD

How I've loved you, Band, through each golden age—
    my earthly heirs to that rare form divine
    in which I clothed my Son! My own image:

mankind—my masterpiece...Christ's love, and mine.
    Your time on Earth you faithfully engage;
    your talents to their highest use align

    my Lucifer to sublimate his rage
in awe of Him whose heart for him, too, bleeds,
    to form his own tribute to God, and gauge

his dire remorse, his deepest human needs
    for fires to thaw Hell's raw and frigid floor.
So, Band. *Your* tribute—Hell himself—now speeds,

    star-lit by art's encouragement to soar,
    to sanctuary in Heaven's golden core.

GOD

Ah, Satan. Have you wearied at long last
of "walking up and down upon the Earth"—
of "going to and fro in it"? The vast

knowledge man pursues, accrues to his worth
not at all—not even one iota small,
until he has learned charity. Your birth

in Christ, till then, cannot burst its caul
and fight its way to light. The Band have learned
charity. Have you, Satan, since your fall,

learned to value righteousness, once so spurned?
And learned at last to know self-righteousness
(to exalt God, through their art, not self, they yearned)

from your own idolized unrighteousness?
Ah, Lucifer! You may yet pass your test.

LUCIFER

Oh, God! Listen to the solemn death knell
of Satan's Hell, as all long-dead throw off
their own oppressive headstones—and my spell.

While I, somehow, can hardly bear to doff
humanity, whose sad-sweet/mortal fate
I covet—good and bad! Judgment, I quaff.

Both time—and Hell—on Earth must now abate.
But life as man, whose joy over pain abounds....
Oh, to stay arrayed in man's "spirited" estate!

Joyful though anguished, my human heart pounds.
I swear by Christ (who man—myself—believes
serves him/my sinners/me!) to God my hope redounds.

Father, forgive me! My human soul grieves,
this day, to be in paradise—with thy thieves.

GOD

Your new humility is not untoward—
for Hell's renunciation, your judgment,
and Heaven's absolution, your reward.

Archangel mine, your prize: as I sent
Christ my Son, as man, to save the world, so
I now send you—upon mankind's art spent—

to save your soul and those in Hell below.
How, now, fallen one—too art-stunned to hear
your art is to raise the lowest of the low?

Christ died that man—even *you*, do not fear—
from His ascension may once again start
new life in paradise. Lucifer, come here!

I kiss you, my prodigal, and thereby impart
to all Hell—*mercy*—my own highest art.

GOD
(turning to the Band)

   Labor, like virtue, is its own sweet reward,
      yet Heaven is surely yours—face to face
with *God*, to whose bosom art drove you so hard.

My Band—who have mirrored, for men to trace,
      my ideal spirit for the world to see—
   without your flaming fame, lit by my grace,

   your gifted light—your art—reflecting me,
man might have lost both his way and his sight,
      forgot his hunger and his thirst for me.

   You have shown pity for my fallen knight
      whose oath upon my Son, body and wine,
restores him and his from their hellish plight.

      For this loving service to me and mine
   I give you your loves, as *my* love the sign.

                        (the Band's Loves are now made
                          fully manifest   in joyful reunion
                        with the grateful artists, poets)

GOD

Sweet Francis—spirit of my Holy Spirit!
So many souls your stubborn love retrieves.
Although but once—in Mary—my word incarnate

conceived my Son, through you this band receives
my triune love—for Lucifer to hear,
whispered in his ear, till he too believes.

Francis—say to your wondering band so dear
how wondrously God's choices are upheld:
saint, my Spirit to instill; man to serve as seer;

sinner, to atone for repentant souls felled,
no longer in Hell's last torment to weep.
Tell them how God's great love for man has swelled

beyond all due to rescue His lost sheep.
So wide God's love for man abides...so deep....

ST. FRANCIS

O dearly human Band—who struggle so to ban
      humanity! I see you look askance
that *your* God would even glance—at Satan.

You knew, O favored few, He would advance
      His judgment to the benefit of all.
But where has He then, you may ask perchance,

when men on Earth cried out—after the Fall,
heirs to crimes unspeakable, of man against man...
where, oh where was He? Ah! From bitterest gall,

Christ, upon the cross, drew strength *His* faith to fan!
      Mercy—sans pareil/Love—par excellence.
These are the differences between God and man.

Devils must kneel to feel this *différence,*
and men must rise to *His* high renaissance.

DANTE

So...we learn, at last—Christianity—
its meaning as it turns "love" into *Love:*
to love our friends more than ourselves, enemy

far more than friend, and *God*—all else above.
It's true; we loved not wisely but too well
(more flesh than spirit—our Circean dove!)—

Earth, her sensual joys...life—its worldly spell....
Now we've learned forgiveness, by Heaven's light.
But how—unless we, too, leave vengeance to Hell—

can we, proselytes, say we won that fight
by which we would uphold the worth of man?
Thus far our souls (and allegory bright)

full circle come: from Heaven where all began—
to Earth...through Hell...and home to Heaven again.

EPILOGUE

(in which The Holy Spirit—appearing to each artist and poet, and to the newly restored, repentant Archangel Lucifer as well, as a miraculous mirrored image not only of his God but of himself: his own highest and best, triumphantly realized self—welcomes the Band, Lucifer, Saint Francis, Jesus Christ, and Man to Heaven at last)

VI

THE HOLY SPIRIT

Most gracious, grace-full vanguards of mankind!
Are you dismayed to find, however dear,
yourselves to *Heaven's* glories now consigned?

I know, my Band, your deepest human fear—
that Heaven, more than Earth, may obviate
your will to serve your God. Dry every tear!

Your need to worship God shall not abate
your passion to still praise Him with your *art*.
I see you stare through me to Heaven's gate,

eager to learn its secrets and to start.
Dear Band, God's kingdom always was entwined
within you. And deep in your deepest heart

God wills you, still, to *create*—so to bind
Him ever deeper, deeper in your mind.

VII

THE HOLY SPIRIT

O Lucifer! You who are now *pro*-Christ—
daring at last confess, as King to Paul:
I am persuaded, saint and man, for Christ—

to say farewell to Hell, God stay my fall...
Satan, you are our true Christian convert—
anxious to *be,* not play, our rebel Saul.

Your worst fear too, like man's, I shall avert:
fear of that second death—of hope to climb
to regain Heaven, all Hell to revert—

for this is surely your last gift of time.
God, Himself, you wrestled. Now, fate forsworn,
you shall atone not only for your crime

but for all your sinners, this holy morn.
To set man right, with Christ, you are reborn.

VIII

THE HOLY SPIRIT

Francis, your prayer for pardon now assigns
peace—*fin de la guerre*—to Armageddon,
as your light-hearted, joyous air reminds

Satan of God's love, though he fought to shun
his craving for that love, which—like the Band's
longing for their art—had to be rewon.

Though dreams of Heaven dimmed through time's last sands
by earthly visions never more adored,
the Band—awed that *you* dared to join hands,

kiss and embrace those lepers all abhorred—
loved Lucifer, despite his deviltry,
teaching him in turn to revere his Lord.

So—*mon soldat* for Christianity...
we win the war for man's humanity.

IX

THE HOLY SPIRIT

Christ Jesus—Thou, God's divine Messiah,
enunciated in Thy word to man
three questions, of awesome, subtle and dire

portent—when salvation's choice is at hand:
Judas, would you betray me with a kiss?
Saul, Saul, why do you persecute me? and

What shall it profit you to gain Earth's bliss
if, in so doing, you shall lose your soul?
Devil, saint and man cannot go amiss—

pondering this profound and pregnant poll.
Thus God stands revealed in His natural bent
to bring men to their ever-lasting goal,

forgiving Hell's most piteous suppliant,
sealing anew with man His covenant.

X

THE HOLY SPIRIT

Man, you've learned more than you dreamed you could:
to believe as if faith shall conquer all,
to labor as if works for God's great good

alone provide the answer to His call.
To know God's grace grants your reuniting
with all you hold most dear on Earth's fair mall,

to show your art (of love) as so inviting
that even Hell's repellent heart must thaw.
So you, like Paul's Christ-impassioned writing,

now reconcile Judeo-Christian law.
For God so loves this world, His own Son, and
man, He forgives your gravest human flaw—

swearing to you/you to your fellow-man:
I love you. Please—love me. I know you can.

ABOUT THE AUTHOR

Patricia Anne Kirby Craddock was born in Atlanta, Georgia. Graduate of The Academy of St. Genevieve-of-the-Pines in Asheville, North Carolina, she attended Georgia State College for Women (Milledgeville) and Oglethorpe University. A founding member of the Georgia State Poetry Society, she is a member of the Poetry Society of America and the Academy of American Poets. In 1982, she was elected a Life Fellow of the International Academy of Poets, Cambridge, England.

www.ingramcontent.com/pod-product-compliance
Lightning Source LLC
LaVergne TN
LVHW091303080426
835510LV00007B/367